BLACK **INK**

Published in the United States by J.iNK Publishing, LLC

Printed in the United States of America
First paperback edition October, 2021

ISBN 978-1-7371075-0-7 (paperback)
ISBN 978-1-7371075-1-4 (ebook)

Book design by Studiolo Secondari
Cover design by Terri Smira for Studiolo Secondari

www.j-ink.com

p 10 9 8 7 6 5 4 3 2 1

BLACK INK

Jabari Khalfani

MY BODY OF WORK

Unveiled and exposed
Adorned in royal antiquity.
Ratchet yet Holy.
Cut from the same cloth
Nat Turner used to wipe his brow.
Tatted with pain and fearlessness.
Bruised and healed by love.
Chiseled with insight and depth.
I present my body...
Unfiltered nakedness.
Charred by flames of justice.
Fashioned nobly after the Divine.
Contemplated on enemy front lines.
Conceived on the oppressor's battlefield.
Formed in the fiery womb of struggle.
Fed from the umbilical cord
Of rebellion.
Ascending from the creative
birth Canal of ingenuity.
And naturally birthed
in the mind of the reader!

— Jabari N. Khalfani

Contents

Part 3 Love

To the Reader:

Thank you kindly for your support and engagement.

Black Ink was inspired by decades of poetry written on envelopes, pamphlets, flyers, and scrap paper lying around. This book is the product of years of emptying my thoughts and perfecting my rhyme scheme. This book is the summation of my lived experiences interpreted and conveyed with fearlessness and conviction.

As you read this book, you'll see that it is separated into three sections: Inspiration, Struggle, and Love. This isn't a coincidence; it speaks to the book's purpose: to educate people of all races, classes, genders, and ethnicities about the struggles and challenges that African-Americans face. As well as foster the realization that this battle is linked to the same struggle for recognition and empowerment of oppressed people of color globally. This book seeks to artistically expose injustices, while inspiring and daring current and future generations to manifest the change they wish to see in the world.

This work presents love in the context of love for self; to inspire self-confidence and self-esteem. Love is further explored within the scope of Black love and the struggles inherent in such relationships. Love is poetically developed and expressed with the goal of healing the wounds of a people who have been deprived of their worth and humanity. As such the words have been spiritually inspired by the countless Black writers, thinkers, philosophers, theologians and poets on whose shoulders I stand. Crafted and composed with intense life-giving energy, this book serves as a healing agent, diminishing all strife and brokenness, while perpetuating holistic health as each word is read. May the prestige and honor of a people be restored, starting chiefly with the Black Queen.

BLACK **INK**

PART 1 **INSPIRATION**

ENIGMA

Superseding
Statistics
And
Stereotypical
Stigmas,
Not just
A Nigga
We're
An enigma,

Our Roots
Can be
Traced,
To Ancient
Empires
Heads of
State,
Our mental
Landscape,
Greater
Than
Alexander
the Great,
They try
And
denigrate,
Make
No mistake,

We're
Descendants
Of
Kings
And
Queens
Not
Planet
of
The Apes,
There's
no debate.

Superseding
Statistics
And
Stereotypical
Stigmas,
Not just
A Nigga
We're an enigma.

They had
Their moment
Momentarily,
Overlooked
Our History
Ordinarily,

Curse
Our customs
Customarily,
Couldn't Hide
Our legends
Too legendary.
All this
Royalty
Hereditary,
Disturbing
Our peace
Unnecessarily,
But if
Necessary,
Our tactics
Vary,
And
We'll
become
Very,
Revolutionary.
While
superseding
Statistics
And
Stereotypical
Stigmas,
Because
We're
Not just
A Nigga
We're
An enigma.

BIOGRAPHY POEM

If the sex was
immaculate
When I was conceived,
is it reasonable to
believe,
That I am an
Immaculate
conception?
Stereotyped to be
lesser
Due to my
complexion,
Deception!
Quite perplexing,
But understood
After reflecting.
Misunderstood
Misconceptions
Which all need
addressing,
So I address it
in this section
Of my biographical
Expression.
Connect the dots
And make connections,
As I connect words
Making more
Poetry selections,
For my collection.
But no more
digression,
Back to the lesson.
Considered at-risk
As an adolescent.
Overcame this
All thanks to
the Omnipresent.
My dad went AWOL.
My Mom remained
Present.
So, I honor her
presence,
No more
storm clouds
Unless I shower her
with presents.
Was ashamed of my
roots,
Now I study my
essence.
Your history is
essential,
knowledge of self
a scarce credential,
Keep this in
remembrance.
Trying to be like God

Excuse the
resemblance.
Youngest of four,
But had a mature
Temperament.
Grew up in a hostile
Environment,
Watching my peers
Die young.
Never seeing
retirement.
Just looking at
imprisonment,
Unfavorable
predicament.
Hoping for their
betterment.
But if you're facing
life in prison,
how is hope even
relevant?
I describe the problem
With great eloquence,
But it still remains
prevalent.
Can't afford to be
hesitant,
Looking to my
President,
All I see
is deception
and incompetence.
How can I be
confident?
Change starts with me!
It's more and more
evident—
Go to
the Black community
If you're looking for
the evidence.
Go back to
school,
Education is
significant.
Doctoral
candidate,
And I'm a willing
participant.

CHASING A DREAM

Lacing
Boots,
Suited
Up
In my
strong suit,
Pressure
Raising,
Heart
Racing,
Victory
Tasting,
Dream
Chasing,
Shirt
Sweaty,
Breathing
Heavy,
Staying
Ready,
Dripping
Sweat,
Seconds
Left,
Game
Time,
Focused
Mind,
Time
To shine,
Victory's
Mine,
Finish Line
Gracefully
Crossed,
Dream Achieved
And Successfully
Caught!

ALL I CAN BE

Back
Being
Better,
Beyond
Being
Broken,
Blissfully
Beaming
Brilliant,
Boy
Better
Believe it!

OUTSIDE THE BOX

Can't be
boxed in.
Mohammed Ali
I come out the box
Boxing.
Cannot
Afford to be locked
Inside the idiot box.
Think outside the box.
Idiot I am not.
Never been
Brainwashed.
So, you hear
a dirty mind
On my soapbox.
I understand
The Game,
So I don't
Play a whole lot.
But the knowledge
I drop,
Keeps me placed
In the penalty box.
Had to get flagrant
My people
Mentally blocked.
keep it Black
Like the
Boondocks.
Take it back
Like a
boom box.
Might sound
Unorthodox.
But I rather
Live freely
Than trapped
In a box!

I'M INSPIRED

Waves crashing
against the beach,
Feeling my stress
Decrease,
As I increase
My peace,
Feeling good
to say the least,
I'm inspired.

Tossed away
All my cares,
Took off
The stress
from the years,
Exchanged it
For new
swimming gear.
Breathing fresh air
While letting
Down my hair,
I'm inspired.

Ocean views
From my room,
Sweet life
In Cancun,
Enjoying the sun
All afternoon,
Fresh fruits
Being consumed.
Spirit aligned,
Mind in tune,
I'm inspired.

Stripped off
my burdens
wearing smiles,
Think I'll stay a while
While
beautiful memories
I Compile.
Chilling in the pool
Meanwhile,
Dropped out
the rat race
too hostile.
"Out The Country"
Status
on
my
Social Media
profile.
Disconnected .
Don't bother
to dial,
I'm inspired.

YES, I AM!

Cool
Naturally,
Created
Wonderfully,
Educated
Masterfully,
Original
Authenticity,
Yes, I Am!
Vibrant
Bold,
Full of
Soul,
Creativity
Explodes,
Melanin
Overload,
Ancestral
Rhythms
Naturally
Flow,
Yes, I Am!
Divine Being,
Dominant Genes,
Original Man,
Permanent
Tan,
Yes, I Am!
Kidnapped
From the
Motherland,
Misunderstood
Too Complex
To Understand,
Respect I Demand,
Proud Black Man,
Yes, I Am!

MELANIN CONFIDENCE

Authentic
Admirable
Audacious,
Boldly
Bodaciously
Black,
Distinctively
Dangerously
Dynamic,
Courageous
Captivatingly
Curvaceous,
Extraordinarily
Eye-catching
Enigma,
Fiery
Feistily
Fierce,
Harmonizing
Healing
Holistic,
Intentional
Iconical
Integral,
Lively
Lovely
Ladylike,
Noble
Natural
Noteworthy,
Passionate
Prominent
Polished,
Ravishing
Remarkable
Royal,
Spectacular
Sensational
Sassy,
Vibrant
Vivid
Vocal...
Never doubts herself or her
abilities. Proudly Embraces her
worth, her looks, full curves, full
lips, Kinky Hair and All.

THOUGHTS AND PRAYERS

In a world full
Of discrimination,
Hatred and
Miseducation,
Remember your past
And destination.
Resist
scandalous
women
And temptation,
Nurture your mind
For elevation.
I pray you find your way.

Maintain balance
through extremes,
Follow dreams
Not fast
money schemes.
Know you're viewed
as a threat
Whenever seen,
Stay out of jail
By any means.
Royalty is in
Your genes,
Keep your
Eyes open
And inner
Vision keen.
I pray you find your way.

Take the lead
Even when behind.
Think
for yourself
Never follow
Blind,
Or you'll
find yourself
Doing time,
Behind bars
Falling further
behind.
Don't father
babies
if you can't
Put pampers
On their
behinds.
I pray you find your way.

Never fold or break,
In a world where
The Black Man's
stress is great.
Keep your
Body, mind
In shape.
Give thanks
Before you sleep
And when you wake,
Don't take
For granted
The breaths
You take.
Provide
Before you
Procreate.
Make sure
It's a Black Queen
Taken
When you take,
Take what's
Rightfully yours
Unapologetically.
Strive to be
A better man
than me.
I pray you find your way.

WHO WILL?

If I don't love her all I can
To avoid her
having a void
To be filled by some
Random man,
Who will?

If I don't allow her to see
How a real man should be,
Who will?

If I don't inspire her dreams
And esteem
Her self-esteem,
Who will?

If I don't treat her
Like a Queen
So she can conceptualize
What it means,
Who will?

If I don't pick her up
When she falls
And give her
The confidence
To stand tall,
Who will?

If I don't say,
Be black
And Unapologetic
Your brown skin
Is Majestic,
Who will?

If I don't plant thoughts
To enrich
So she knows
To get rich
Without being
A vixen,
Who will?

If I'm not around
To experience
Her ups and downs
Help her find herself
When her identity
Can't be found,
Who will?

If I don't stick it out
When things get heated
Not walk away defeated
Who will?
...I will
Because
Real Black Men
Are needed!

A GOOD SPORT

Dear Shorty
Stay sporty.
MVP
No one's
Out your
League.
Gold Medal
Front Runner
Don't Settle.
Coach You
Of course.
Teach you
To excel in life
Not just a sport.
Give you the truth
I won't distort.
You'll always
Have my support.
Don't drop the ball
It's in your court.
Three strikes
You're out
Bad news
For black males
In the Courts.
"When They See Us"
It's a
Blood sport.
So be
A
Good sport.
Take All
That's
Yours
But don't
Take
shorts.
Do something
Hallmark,
Hit it out
the ballpark.
Perfect
your
Game plan,
Hit a
Grand slam.
Give 100%
Do the best
You can.
If you fail

I understand.
I'll always be
Your
biggest fan.
And you'll
Always be
my lil man
And forever...
my Sporty
Dear Shorty!

BOUNCE BACK

Back off the wall
Get back
In the game.
The Harder
you fall
The harder
you train.
When life
Throws
you grapes
you make
Champagne.
Can't appreciate
The sun
without
Storm clouds
And rain.

SETTLE UP

Settle for less?
Not a settler
Author and editor
Use my head
To stay ahead
Of my competitor
Handle business
On my cellular
Never do it
Regular!

CIPHER

Sick train of thought
but my pen game
Is well.
If I raise my pen
I raise hell.
Fire on the pen tip
Like it was demented.
Stand firm
Like my feet
was cemented.
So if I said it
I meant it.
Translator
presented,
To decipher
What I spit
In a cipher.
Happily cooling
But my pen is
Mad Hyper.
breakdown
Heavy topics
That make you
Feel lighter.
Started off
As a nomad
With a notepad,
Because in the
Beginning
It was written,
Need a bib
How I'm spitting.
Humbly slaying
Lyrics
Like a
Gunslinger,
That's a
humdinger.
Retarded flow
But no
Dumb Nigga!

BURGLARY

I rang the bell
I tried to knock,
My efforts failed
Your mind
was locked.
Freeing you
mentally
meant
Illegal Entry.
So I broke
the locks,
The mental
blocks.
Ready to shoot,
An army of troops,
Armed with the truth.
Ready to pick locks
Set off alarms,
Not firearms,
No intended harm.
Home invasion,
Re-education
for
Misinformation,
Entering
your mind
No invitation.
I kicked down
The door.
Now the light
Is exposed,
Your mind
Has been
burglarized
No longer
Closed.

ARE YOU AFRAID OF THE DARK?

Black mixed with Black.
Chocolate covered,
Melanin smothered,
Concentrated
Solution,
No whitening,
No bleaching,
No watering down,
or dilution.
Naturally
from the Earth
No artificial
substitutions.
Are You Afraid of the Dark?

Skin that drips
Honeydew mist,
Hair in
Tight curls
That can't
Untwist,
Thick thighs
Wide hips,
African nose
Full luscious lips,
Golden brown Skin
Divinely Sun-kissed.
Are You Afraid of the Dark?

Mahogany
Drenched in Ebony,
Confident
Essential Condiment,
Angelic embodiment.
Goddess of the ages
she amazes,

All of Nature
sings
Her praises.
Humanity's Mother,
Sweetest Berry
Darkest color,
Queen of
Civilization
Incomparable
To another.
Are You Afraid of the Dark?

Men beg
to hook up
She has them
hooked,
You can look
her over
But she can't

Be overlooked.
Whenever she's near,
She evokes
Intense stares,
Voluptuous breast
Well-endowed rear,
You'll swear.
You must have it,
Creating chocolate addicts,
with severe habits.
Lust in your eyes
Lost in a daze,
withdrawal kicking In
It's her that you crave,
You want to sip
the cocoa
So why are you
Afraid?

SHE AIN'T GOT TIME

Come talking
A mile a minute
You won't
Last a minute.
She's not
About that,
She'll
cut you
Short
A minute flat.
Don't approach
Her
With the
Lame,
Trying to
Gain,
From running
Game.
Soft voice
However,
Attitude
Tough
Like leather,
Better
Have your stuff
Together.
Places to go
Things to do,
Not a minute
To waste
on you.
If your
On joke time,
She'll decline,
You're getting
No time,
Next in line.
In a New York
Minute
She's out of there.
Ain't got time,
Not a minute
to spare.

PART 2 **STRUGGLE**

ANGRY BLACK MALE

What you hide
controls you,
What you don't say
owns you,
Fake a smile
What we're
prone to,
But it's not
What I'm going to.
"Boy"
Is how they
Address me,
They shackle,
Arrest me,
Hang me from trees
Cut off my testes,
How much more
Can they test me?
They want me to
Smile
But how
Can they
Expect me?
They turn around
And blame me,
If I dare get angry.
We've been victims
Of terrorism,
Which is why
I'm so cranky.
My upside-down
smile,
Doesn't mean
I'm hostile,
It just means
I'm healing
And it might
take a while.

BIG CHAINS

Big Chains,
Silver Chains,
Slaves Working
Chain gangs.
Silver Chains
Now Gold-plated,
False symbols
that we made it.

NO BALLERINA

She's just
a balancing act.
Single-Handedly
Shoulders
responsibilities,
she balances that.
Balancing two
jobs Such a
challenge,
Unprotected
Disrespected
Never thrown off-balance.
Putting food
In her kid's mouth,
Even when her
checking accounts
Don't balance out.
Balance of power
Not in her favor,
Society
Betrayed Her,
Weak men
Tried to play her.
She's still
Phenomenal
Won't let that
Intimidate her.
Her pride
under attack,
She wears
her confidence
And
fights back.
Too Strong.
Too Black.
No ballerina
She's just
A balancing act!

BEHIND THE SCENE

Behind the scene,
Royal
African Queen,
Always noticed
Seldom seen,
Degraded
Demeaned,
Should be
esteemed,
Invisible
unseen,
But always there
Behind the scene.

When humans first
appeared,
She was there,
Since B.C.
She was too hot for
AC,
Before Christ,
She was looking nice.
Since antiquity,
Queens like Nefertiti,
Shined vividly,
Whited out
of history,
big old lies

bigotry.
Stripped of all
her dignity,
Now she strips
For the industry,
She's currently
controlled
By currency,
So clarity
Is not a certainty,
But she's behind the
scenes
Certainly.

Behind the scene,
Royal
African Queen,
Always noticed
Seldom seen,
Degraded
Demeaned,
Should be
Esteemed,
Invisible
unseen,
But always there
Behind the scene.
She picked your cotton

Wove your silk,
Raised a nation
On
Blood, sweat, tears
And breast milk.
Thanks to her
The White House
And Capital
Were built.
Queen of D.C.,
Unmistakably.
But they berate her,
As she
Nursed the babies
Of men that raped her.
Snatched
from her home
To become
A homemaker.

It's Been proven,
She mothered
Illegitimate sons
By Founding
Fathers
Of
The Constitution.
Seldom honored for
her
Contribution,
imitated by all
But there's no
substitution.

Behind the scene,
Royal
African Queen,
Always noticed
Seldom seen,
Degraded
Demeaned,
Should be
esteemed,
Invisible
unseen,
But always there
Behind the scene.

FOUR-LETTER WORD

My only crime
Was being
born poor,
Now my chances
of arrest
Are multiplied
by four.

4 times more likely
To be stopped
By police,
4 times more likely
to say
"I can't breathe."

4 times more likely
To be caged
Behind 4 walls,
4 times more likely
To be shot
4 nothing at
all.

4 times the injustice
But no one will stop it,
Free labor in jail
4 times the profit.

BAD BLOOD

It's a blood bank
In the streets,
More blood
being added
As I speak.
The future's
Looking bleak,
Who to blame
For the grief,
The police
Or
neighborhood
beef?

Success
Looks
Far-fetched.
guns sold
On the black market,
Now everything black
Is a target,
to be shot dead
on target,
youngsters
Take their
Last breath,
And their lives
Just started.

It's a war in the streets,
blood flows like a creek,
A mother's heart
is getting weak,
Agony added
As l speak.

It's a blood bank
in the streets
And it's the same
every week.

No
blood transfusions,
only
mass confusion.
Who will clean
the blood and
the other Mass
pollution?
As Black blood

Splatters,
Another Black Life Shattered,
Blacks Get Madder,
Until the whole World
Knows
Black Lives Matter.

It's a war in the streets,
blood flows like a creek,
the stench of dead flesh reeks.
A daughter's heart
is getting weak,
Agony added
As I speak,
And it's the same
every week.

BEING BLACK IS STRESSFUL

Imagine,
Being pulled
Down,
Because his pants
Aren't pulled up.
Police pull
Him over,
Pull out guns,
Pull him down,
Down
to the station.
Now he has to
Pull some strings.
Wish he could
Pull together,
But his kind
Has been
Conditioned
To pull apart.
So now they
Pull triggers.
Baby on the way,
She say
He didn't
Pull out.
Trying to pull
a 9 to 5,
Now he's
pulling double
shifts.
Tried to pull
his Boss
Aside,
But was given
no regard.
Told to work hard,
And stop
Pulling
The race card.
What to do?
He was trying
to pull through,
But with so much
on his plate,
He needed a little
Break,
He can't pull
All the weight.
It's pulling out
his life,
Like someone
pulled out
a knife,

...........collapse

PROMISED LAND

No Lows.
We're high
all the time.
No shining shoes
Only
Our melanin shines.
Eating Grapes
Off the vine,
No Protesting
No Picket Signs.
We're in the Promised Land.

No more killing.
We're protected.
As Men
We're Respected,
Our skin color
And Credit
Are Accepted.
Ghettos gone,
We've Resurrected.
We're in the Promised Land.

No burgers or crack
to flip.
We understand love
And Real
relationships.
She owns
strips of land,
She doesn't need to
Strip.
They love each other
Freely
He doesn't need
To tip.
We're in the Promised Land.

Our thinking is clear.
Our debt is cleared.
We got money
to spare,
No more despair,
Air Pollution
gone
Only love's
in the air.
If such a place exists,
Please take me there.
So I can say,
we're in the Promised Land.

DEFINITION OF A KING

Lion
Lover
Warrior
Comforter,
Classy
Courageous
Godly
Gracious,
Respectful
Royal
Provider
Loyal,
Diligent
Prudent
Teacher
Student,
Go-getter
Perfectionist
Romantic
Affectionate,
Listener
Leader
Open-minded
Reader,
Protector
Father Figure
Supportive
Permanent
Fixture.

A GOOD RUN

A Thug
Redefined,
And Refined,
Touched all
Humankind,
With a
California
state of Mind.

Gang-banger
For starters,
But proved
To Be Smarter,
Left your mark
Like
Permanent
Marker,
Died a Black
Martyr,
Hood's
Obama,
Teacher
Father.

Artistic,
Prolific,
Urban Prophet
To be
More Specific.
Simply Put,
Too complex,
To digest,
Black intellect,
Self-taught
Malcolm X.
When the
Weed Smoke
Cleared,
It was
Clear
You were
A threat,
Assassinated
Broad day
They came
For your neck,
But We
The people
Will never
Forget,
We the
people
Will show
Love
And Respect.

Forever
idolized,
For the hoods
You revitalized,
Gave unusual
hope
To A People
Usually
Marginalized.
You gave
The Hustler's
Blue Print
For youth to
strategize,
Hated
Because your
Mind wasn't
Colonized.

They tried
to end
Your Glory,
Prematurely,
They
Failed Poorly,
Jealousy
Purely,
You'll be
Immortalized
Surely.

Hating the news,
But No More
Crying the blues,
The Entrepreneur,
Wanted Us
To Have More,
So I'm lacing
Up my shoes,
We got work to do,
The Marathon
Continues!
(Rest Easy,
Nipsey Hussle)

HOW MANY KINGS

How many Kings
Have we lost?
I think
I lost the count.
Countless Kings
before him
A Ridiculous amount.
Countless Kings
After him
Too many to discount.
Another King
was shot.
Another King
Was got....
But Countless Kings
won't Surrender Our
Legacy
won't stop!

FOCUS

Can I just focus
On being great?
Without being
The focus
Of your
Stereotypes
And
hate.

Focused
on beating odds
Many brothers
Didn't beat,
Trying to stay out
the focus
Of Guns and police.

The News
Report us
As hopeless,
So I'm constantly
Switching my focus.

"Focus on Money"
Is what they say to do,
Hard to focus on yourself
When Black Lives
Are devalued.

Negativity and wrong
Is all they
focus on,
so I have to go within,
to find the courage
To keep focusing.

MISTAKEN IDENTITY

Looking
Seeking,
Searching
Peeking.
Where does
her
Beauty start?
Where does it
Stop?
Who is she really?
Who is she
really not?
Hunting
Searching,
Looking for that
inner person.
The one who
deserves,
To be defined
in her
Own words!

THESE EYES...

These Eyes...
Are windows to a world
that I dare not stare at too long.
For beauty and sorrow
can be seen in a blink of an eye.

These Eyes...
Have to remain closed at times.
For what l see can deceive me.
I must keep a blind eye to
Coonery
and buffoonery,
which are easily distracting.

These Eyes...
Are not limited to 20/20 vision.
Instead I use insight and
foresight
to see past stereotypes.

These Eyes...
Can never forget what they saw,
for pain, bigotry and injustice
should never be overlooked.

These Eyes...
have learned to see beyond
the limited views others have of
me.
They only see parts of me.
They lack true Vision.

These Eyes...
Do not define my complete
reality.
As I am not restricted to what my
eyes can see.
By faith I lay hold on that which
my eyes
have not seen.

These Eyes...
Reflect my highest, greatest self
that I gaze at with pride and
admiration.
I can't let someone's small
thinking of me
be projected onto my greatness

These Eyes...
Accept all
that my eyes can see.
Just plain old amazing me.
No editing, no filtering,
Nappy hair and all.
Exceptionally ordinary
and wonderfully made.

GRAVITY CHECK

Gravity Check, Gravity Check,
Do my Air Jordans make me fly?
Or am I still shackled
Regardless of how many pairs
I buy?

Gravity Check, Gravity Check,
Folks pull themselves down
to sleeping on the street,
Just to say they had them first
When a new pair is released.

Gravity Check, Gravity Check
Blew your whole check,
Reality check,
You still
Black and Oppressed.
You ain't fly
Just buried in debt.
If you want to spread your wings
First elevate your mindset!

BUSINESS MAN

Business man
No business plan,
A slave to wealth
No knowledge
Of self.

Business man
No business plan,
Got big dreams,
Got big schemes,
Getting that green,
By any means.

Business man
No business plan,
Work for the man?
He refused,
Taking unnecessary risk
Didn't pick and choose,
Needed it quick,
Nothing to lose.

Business man
No business plan,
Took to the streets,
Trying to make
Ends meet,
Wasn't discreet,
Got caught
By Police.

Business Man
Your business plan,
Is incomplete,
Needs to be
Tweaked,
Revised, Delete,
Thinking
Shallow,
Got you in
Trouble
Knee-deep!

TEN YEAR CHALLENGE

Then and Now
Still the same,
Still in the same
orange suit
And chains.
Just a number
They have
no name,
1 in 5
black males
Lives this pain.
Blacks & Whites
Do crimes
the same,
But Blacks
get sentenced for
longer time frames.
Insane
Inhumane,
The justice system
Is to blame,
Take the challenge,
Make a change!

BLANK

Trying to fit in
Where you don't
Belong,
Holding hands
Singing songs,
Going along
To get along.
Trying to right
The past
By overlooking
The wrongs,
As if
your
memory
Bent
Blank...

They weren't
Shooting
Blanks
Or playing
games,
When
Blacks
Are shot
and killed
At point
Blank
range.

Do Black
Lives Matter?
What do
You think?
Look at
History,
Fill in the
Blank?

But there's
Nothing to
dispute,
The
Blank
Pages
Are the
proof.
We were
Blanked
Out of
History
Guess
They never
Gave a
Blank...
And that's
The point
Blank
Truth!

NO BLASPHEMY

Was it blasphemy
When they
imprinted
false images
On my mentality?
Got me
rethinking
God
And spirituality.
In reality,
Seeing God
in Your own likeness
Is a matter of
Practicality.
Some say God
Has no color,
In actuality,
It has always
been Alright,
As long as God
Was colored White.
That's where
I have a gripe,
Lies colored white,
We must
blackout and rewrite,
Out of the darkness
comes the light.
How could Christ
Be risen,
And the truth
Still hidden?
Fill my cup
Until Melanin's
Over dripping,
God in Color,
More befitting.
How could
A cross appear,
With no color there,
When every
Black man
Has a cross
To bear?

COLORS

Life is a box of crayons
"Get the Green"
Is what they say.
You can do no wrong
If you're White,
And
Justice is still
Gray.
Make sure
Your colors are true,
Whatever you do,
Because
Black and Brown
Are killed
By those
In Blue.
Why sweat
to make
your daily bread?
Instead,
Look for
A yellow-
Brick road
To get Ahead.
But most of us
Die searching
While our finances
remain in the Red!

MONKEY BUSINESS

Monkey see
Monkey do,
Should I be racist
And imitate you?
Bring that Monkey Business
We will run you out of town,
Guerrilla warfare
It's going down.
No more monkeying around.
Was trying to keep cool
And relax,
But had to get
The monkeys
Off my back!

CONCRETE JUNGLE

Welcome to
the Concrete Jungle
AKA
the Ghetto,
Where Cries
of
Hungry children
echo,
Luxury homes
on the outskirts,
with plush
Green
Meadows.

Vegetation
down,
Rent raised
high,
overgrown
buildings
Touching
Polluted
skies.

Safari
of a
different
kind,
bullets pouring
Rain or shine,
Where
Being black
Equals crime,
And
Black Males
Are hunted
All the time.

Competitive,
harsh,
a rumble
for resources,
A million men
March.

Black mammals
Roam wasted,
Wasting their life
In a wasteland,
Ready to waste
His own kind
on a dime,
Gun in waistband.

.

Cell phone
Towers
Make us
sickly,

Fed
A
Fast Food
Diet
strictly,
Police
Kill Us
Slowly,
Genocide
Occurring
Quickly.

Government
Swamped,
beyond
polluted,
No Health care
for the
wounded,
the Poor
Have been
excluded,
the system
ill-suited,
Needs to be
Uprooted.
.
Less wildlife
only
Wild night,
Tears of drear
Form rivers
here,
Caged prisons
readily
appear,
Addressing
Overpopulation
Fears,
But
The struggles
continue,
Every lion
Wants his share!

THE REVOLUTION

The Revolution
Will be recorded
On an iPhone.

The Revolution
Will be Uploaded
to YouTube
And World Star.

The Revolution
Will go viral.

The Revolution
Will be retweeted.

The Revolution
Will have
Millions of likes
And
Memes.

The Revolution
Will be
Photoshopped,
with
SnapChat filters.

The Revolution
Won't happen.
Social media
Has our attention!

CATCH YOUR BREATH

Breathe out
slow
Relax more
easily,
Exhale stress
Raise your
frequency,
Big Deep
breaths
Inhale
More
Frequently,
Repeat this
Repeatedly,
Experience
Life more
Peacefully.

PART 3 **LOVE**

INK SECRETIONS

Wrapping my naked fingers
On your body,
firmly pressing against
Your lower torso.
Fingers stroking
Your sleek black frame.
Rocking you back and forth
making sure
fluids flow,
And you're ready to go.
I feel the tip
It's moist
And
Needs no moistening.
I lay your body
On the paper pallet
Magically,
You squirt
passionately.
Dancing
In rhythmic, riveting, rising
motions,
Turning white paper to blue
oceans.
The product of our chemistry
Penetrate staining the paper
Permanently,
As we engage in bizarre
uniformity.
History will show
we had relations...
The proof will be
Ink Secretions!

JUST LOOKING

I peep
You peep
We like to peep
When we're alone.

We have to peep
How we're peeping
There's others
In our zone.

No sloppiness,
Nothing obvious,
Something discreet
As a peep.

I know
You know,
Others can't
Peep it though.

I peeped
You wearing
My favorite skirt,
And you peeped
Me flexing
in your
favorite shirt.

You peeped
How I sneaked
From my significant
other,
So we could have time
To peep at each
other.

I wonder
You wonder
Who's peeping
Who now,
But because of our vows.
More peeping isn't allowed.

We seem to have
This peeping
thing down,
Because no one
sees us
Peeping around.

But lately,
We've been
seeking
Additional time
For
Additional peeping,
Others have peeped
And said we are cheating,
But in our minds
We're only peeping.

LOVE IS STILL BEAUTIFUL

Love is still beautiful
Or so I thought.
Love teaches
Hard lessons,
I've been taught.
You want it,
Gotta fight,
So I fought,
Put down
My guard
Heart got caught,
Heart got broken,
Cut left open,
Love is still beautiful
Still I'm hoping.

DO YOU BELIEVE IN LOVE?

We once stood
Joyfully,
in the splendor of our
Royalty.
Our love was pure and
vibrant,
As we rightfully ruled our
environment.
Our Black Love was
Cemented,
And positively
Represented.
This went on
For centuries,
Some of our fondest
Memories.
But inner conflict
And Enemies
Tragically
Disrupted our
Legacy.
Now we don't
Embrace
Our Culture
or
Identity.
Finding it difficult
To relate,
going outside
our race
To Date,
Perpetuating
Self-hate.
Has Black Love
Lost its meaning?
Why is "Black"
So demeaning?
What has our crowns
Leaning,
Instead
of Beaming?
Why do we harbor
Negative
feelings?
We're in
desperate need
Of
Healing.

Let's end
The
Negative trend
so
Unappealing.
Let's make
Amends,
Black Love
Restored
Again,
For this
I Am
Pleading.

GODLY ENCOUNTER

The heavens didn't open.
No parting of the clouds;
No Caucasian male descending
No, that's not how.

No walking on water of any kind.
No turning water into wine.
No cross or crucifixion,
Not even a mere church sign,
one could find.

Her presence was Angelic.
Not the God
from Sunday school,
But her Godliness
authentic,
consumed by her essence,
every moment relished.

Blessed with African Pride,
rare and distinct
Her divinity undenied,
Voluptuous
Curvaceous
Difficult to describe.
From the heavens she derived.

Awed and amazed,
Majestic elegance for days,
Her burning bush sets my soul
ablaze.
Her holiest place I seek to lay,
With plans to delay my stay.

Transformed by her presence,
Utopia reached in seconds,
This had to be God
The feeling too pleasant!

MELANIN QUEEN

Earthly Melan,
sweet
like watermelon.
Fill my cup,
let it
Overflow.
Native Melan,
Juicy fruity Melan,
Sipping
As its dripping
good for my soul,
makes me whole.
Radiant Melan,
dazzling Melan,
mesmerized
by her essence,
Graced
By her presence.
Vibrant
Pigment
Pronounced
Profound,
organic compounds,
trickling down.
Chocolate DNA
Darkening the Milky Way,
Heading Straightaway,
To your gateway.

Fervent Feelings Fester,
Nothing could be better,
Than
Tasting the Neter
In her Nectar.
Melanin being
Melanin Queen,
Glory and Splendor,
Beyond measure.
To taste your fruit
Is to taste the truth,
How I treasure,
to endeavor

A BODY OF KNOWLEDGE

Her body
enticed me,
Ways she moved
Kept me glued,
Her sexiness
spicy,
burning images
On my
psyche,
undoing
them
unlikely.

Shortness of breath,
the effect,
of her wearing
A short dress,
Curves that had
depth
she possessed
Voluptuous thighs
in excess,
And the best
of the best,
Plump
ravenous
Breast.

Perky ripe cutie,
Like gossip
she's juicy,
Plentiful hips
phenomenal booty,
succulent lips
undeniable beauty.

Transparent,
No
Falsehood,
She
most certainly
could,
Stiffen
my wood,
But she
Stimulated
More
Than
My manhood,
Yes,
she was
Damn good.

Her body
was edible,
soft as a whisper,
Truly unforgettable.

But her mind
More
incredible,
thoughts
More Intelligible,
Making her
More eligible,
Instant Attraction
inevitable.

Articulate
expression,
and
Reflective
Reflections,
Proved
Her intellect,
Was as
Sexy
As
Her other
Assets,
Positive
Impression
left,
Without
her
Getting
undressed,

A body
of
knowledge
one should
invest.

FLEXIBLE

She Loves
And
does
me right,
flexible
And
loose
Never
cranky
Or uptight.

Warm welcomes
When
I call,
rides me
superb
Without
Riding my
nerves,
Her
regular
Protocol,
Allowing me
To squeeze
As I please,
As
her Feet
touch
the wall.

Stretching
My imagination
with
the passion
readily
produced,
She stretched
her legs
And I'm
seduced,
If I'm stiff
She gets
Me loose.

Respectful
When we
Interact,
Never
says, "I can't
Do that."
She's flexible
And bendable,
She knows
how to adapt.

BLUSHING

Rock my melanin
Like Jewels
So I'm usually cool,
Cooling like December,
As I
Try to
remember,
To keep
A cool temper,
But every time
I look at her,
She raises
My Temperature.
Her lips
Her hips
Her sway
Her switch,
Her Sexy mischief,
Got me
Losing
my cool
Where's
my handkerchief?
Didn't feel
the need
to toughen,
But as soon
As she starts
touching,
My toughness
softens
like muffins,
blood rushing,
Sensations
Gushing,
On her
I'm crushing,
And
Even though
I'm chocolate
I start blushing,
Yes,
I'm blushing!

THE FIRST KISS

Excited from the touch
lips begin to brush,
Sensations Rush,
Manhood
Mans up.
Kisses dealt,
Passion felt,
Time is still
Spine is chilled.
Fireworks spark
Intensity starts,
Mouthparts
Can't pull apart.
Mesmerized,
Feeling butterflies,
bliss
In every
Crevice of her
lips.
How I Reminisce,
On that first
Kiss.

CASUAL CONVERSATION

HIM: I've been mining for
diamonds,
And I've been digging you for
weeks.

HER: Your vision's small,
I've seen it all.

HIM: You're confusing me,
To what you usually see,
You could choose to be
Happier
By choosing me!

HER: Happiness begins with
me,
Truthfully,
On my own I can grow
fruitfully,
I can stand alone,
No recruiting me.

HIM: If laughter is
medicine
Medically I'm credible,
My medicine impeccable,
Sensation Sensual,
Nibbling on your earlobes
as if they're edible,
feeling electrical,
The reaction chemical,
Ecstasy inevitable!

HER: Nice with the words,
So I observe,
Amazed,
How you Set my Soul ablaze,
Got me Observing You Like
Holidays!

HIM: Good observation,
Time to Bear Down On Barriers,
Commence the penetration.

HER: Heavy flirtation,
With high Expectations,
Creates a situation
of overstimulation,
Moving too fast
might get a citation,
Slow your row
Bro,
No more Casual
conversation.

HEALTHY SNACK

You're Healthy
And a snack.
My Good
And Juicy,
Healthy snack.
Don't mind
The calories,
Too tasty
To count,
Savory
And
Mouthwatering
Too good
To eat
in small
Amounts.

Consuming
For hours,
Greedily
Devour,
Appetite
Excessive,
Returning
For seconds,
Too Good
For a Quickie,
Things get
Sticky,
Licking
My
Fingertips
And lips,
As your
Nectar
drips.

I indulge
Till I bulge,
So amazing
Misbehaving,
A continuous
Craving,
Connection
Stronger than
Bluetooth,
Satisfying
My Sweet tooth,
Awesomeness
Deliciousness,
I make a mess,
But could
Care less,
Too busy
Trying to
eat Healthy!

LOVER AND A FIGHTER

It was either fight or
flight,
and flight didn't seem
right,
so I'm committed
outright,
even when it's an uphill
fight.
Fighting off distractions should they ever come in
sight,
Fighting through tough times, challenges force us to
unite.
We don't fight amongst ourselves, so dysfunction ain't our
plight,
but if by chance we end up
fighting
May it be an opportunity to become more
enlightened
through our
strife,
Excelling to higher
heights,
Knowing it will all be worth the
price,
If we don't give up the
fight.

BABY GOT BACK

If I'm
in trouble
I call her
for backup,
If I stumble
or fumble,
She helps me
back up.

No acting up,
She breaks
it down
And backs
it up.

Won't turn
her back,
Won't stab
my back,
No dirt
Behind
my back,
She has
my back,
Simple as that.

Helps me
on my feet
When I
fall short,
she has
my back
That's
back support.

Argue
back
and forth
no time
For that,
that's ass
backwards
Too fine
for that,
we take a loss
we bounce
Right back,
until we get
back on track.

Challenges
Come around,
She won't
back down,
since back
in the day
it's been
Like that,
We're going
Forward
Cuz we go
back!

MY ROCK

If I'm between a rock and a
hard place
she helps me to rock on,
She's rock solid for me to
count on,
She's My Rock!

If hard times rock my
foundation,
Or if I hit rock bottom and in
a bad
Situation,
She'll rock it out with me
regardless of what I'm
facing
She's My Rock!

Get my rocks off for one
night of
swerving,
That's not how I'm rocking
she's much more
deserving,
Put a rock on her finger so
you know it's
For certain,
She's My Rock!

Rock steady
through the ages,
Rock the house
until we're rocking grand
babies,
And
When my song come
on,
We'll be rocking all night
long,
And if I get rock hard ain't
nothing
Wrong,
because
She's My Rock!

BOOM, BOOM, BOOM!

Hitting harder than
speakers knock,
She rocks me
right out
My socks,
You can hear
Her vibes
coming down
the block,
Boom, Boom, Boom!

Her energy
Captures me,
I freely surrender
Don't set me free,
No other place
I'd rather be,
Than in your
Proximity,
The sweetest melody,
Boom, Boom, Boom!

She Radiates,
And Vibrates,
My Mental State
She Stimulates,
My inner vibe
She elevates,
like
Boom, Boom, Boom!

Pedigree
heavenly,
feeling
Incredibly,
Interest
Increasing
Steadily,
It's that
Boom, Boom, Boom!

Although it's potent,
I keep sipping her
potion,
headfirst
I dive into her ocean,
Perfect stroke in motion,
Excuse the ruckus
and commotion,
it's just that
Boom, Boom, Boom!

IN MY ARMS

Let me
rock you
Close to my chest.
Rock away
Your stress,
Your pains
And bitterness.
You can rest
And feel refreshed,
With my sweet
Caress.
You're Safely wrapped
In my arms.

No more
Being left
Unprotected.
Dignity,
Royalty,
No more
Being
disrespected.
You deserve
The best
So let me
Give you
What's expected.
I know
We haven't
Always come
correct,
But that's
All being
Corrected.
And loving you
Perfect
Is being
perfected.
Now that
You're safely wrapped
In my Arms.

I'm asking
Forgiveness,
And God
Bear me witness.
We Overlooked
Your beauty,
Neglected
Our rightful
duty.
Exploited you
for boobs
And booty.
Labeled you
Unruly,
If you dared
Act

moody.
Were we wrong?
Absolutely,
But love
Can heal
the wrong
and cruelty.
And we can
continue loving
with greater
continuity.
So come
Get loved
By yours
Truly.
You're safely wrapped
In my Arms

LOST

I lose track of time
When I'm lost in your
vibe.
At a loss for words
because I'm lost in your
eyes.
Awed and amazed,
lost in a daze,
By the swerve of your curves
And
How your sexiness sways.

Lost in the moment
since the first time we
dated.
My focus was lost
In memories we
created.
I'd rather be lost in your love
Than lost without
you,
My African Queen
My Melanin
Honeydew.
Had others in the past,
but they all lost
to you.
Almost lost you
one time,
And I almost lost
my mind.
Can't afford to lose you,
Good women
are hard to find.
Forever lost in your sauce
Is exactly what I'm choosing,
Because when you're
Rolling with a winner
There really is no losing.

SAVING GRACE

In a cold and sinful world
My only desire
is saving Grace.
Lead me to your altar
of redemption.
Let me kneel
At your bodacious throne.
Unveil your sanctified body
So I can eagerly partake
In sweet Communion.
How I long to sip of the divine juice
Which Only your body can produce.
Feed me from the fruit of
Your loins.
Baptize me in your holy water and
Secretion.
Nurse away my sorrows
In your bosom.
Pour out your passionate spirit
Until I transcend into an
Orgasmic eternity.
Fill me with your Salvation
Until I burst with joyful bliss.
Drown me in your river Jordan
So I can experience
Heavenly paradise
and be born again.
A refreshed New
Man.

STORYBOOK LOVE

She's my storybook love,
One of her many titles.
True love she illustrates
And it's always colorful and vivid.
I don't judge her by her cover
I read her under the covers,
From cover to cover,
Paying close attention
To her ideas and details.
I open her up
And travel into new dimensions.
I put her on my lap
Stroking and fingering through her pages.
Licking my fingers as the pages turn.
A closed book to some
But she opens up to me.
I absorbed everything she wrote
Hanging on to her every quote.
She doesn't deserve to be on a shelf
So I place her gently in my hands.
She's a book I can't put down
So I praise her and lift her up.